Ben 10: 2018
A CENTUM BOOK 978-1-911460-76-3
Published in Great Britain by Centum Books Ltd
This edition published 2017
1 3 5 7 9 10 8 6 4 2

BEN 10, CARTOON NETWORK, the logos, and all related characters and elements are trademarks of and © Cartoon Network. (s17)

No part of this publication may be reproduced, stored in a retrieval system, or transmitted in any form or by any means, electronic, mechanical, photocopying, recording or otherwise, without the prior permission of the publishers.

Centum Books Ltd, 20 Devon Square, Newton Abbot, Devon, TQ12 2HR, UK

books@centumbooksltd.co.uk

CENTUM BOOKS Limited Reg. No. 07641486

A CIP catalogue record for this book is available from the British Library

Printed in China.

centum

BEN 10

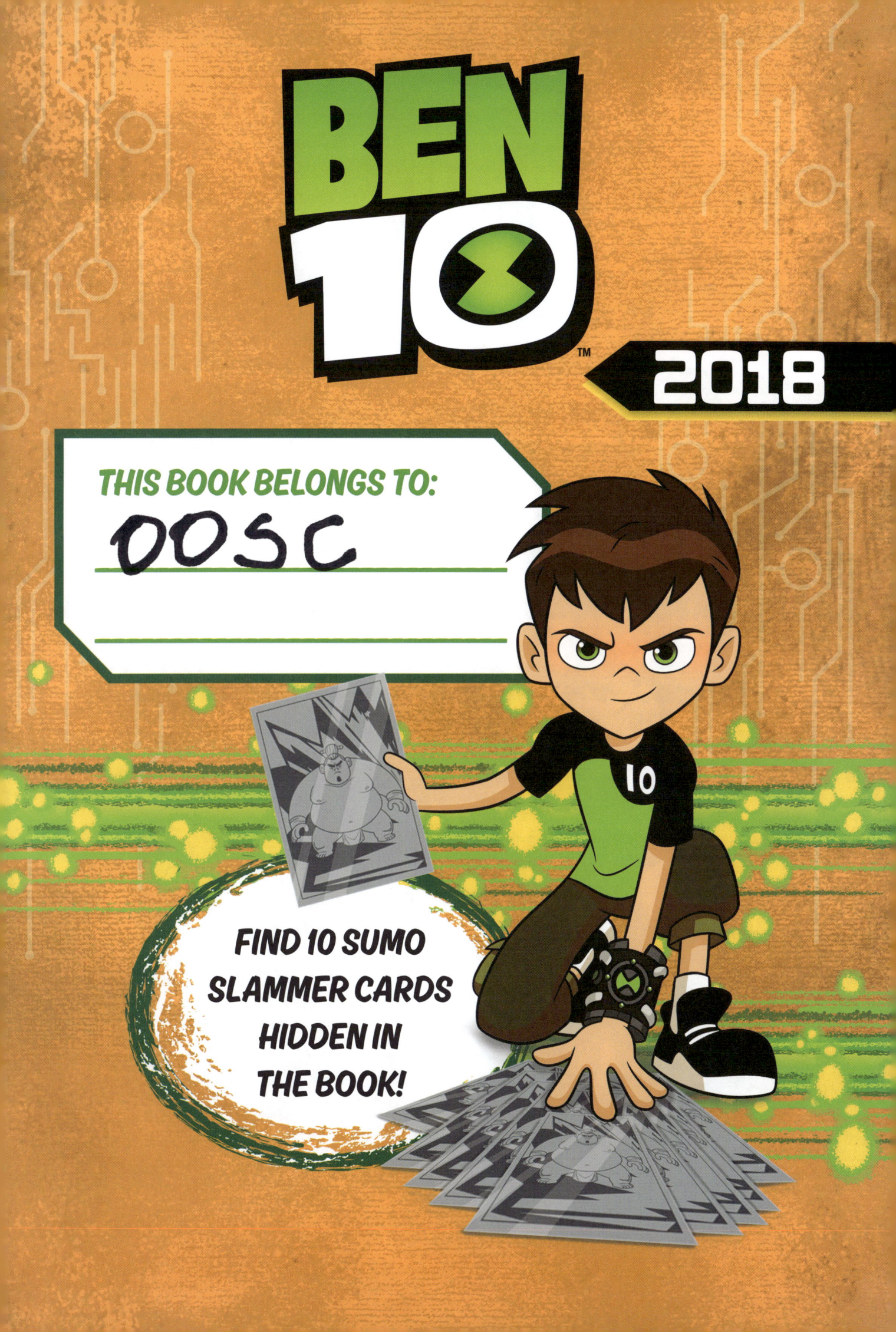

2018

THIS BOOK BELONGS TO:
OOSC

FIND 10 SUMO SLAMMER CARDS HIDDEN IN THE BOOK!

WELCOME, ADVENTURE SEEKERS!

Ben and Gwen's epic summer trip with Grandpa Max in the Rustbucket continues with more hikes, museum trips, villains to battle and infinite fun.

Everything changed when Ben found the Omnitrix, now he can transform into any of ten aliens, each with their own unique powers.

You can read about their powers on the fact pages throughout the book. Plus there are loads of fun activities, puzzles, art challenges and stories for you to get stuck into.

But first let's meet everyone...

Rustbucket

Ben

Gwen

Grandpa Max

HERE COME THE ALIENS!

Grey Matter — Page 36

Wildvine — Page 47

Diamondhead — Page 24

Overflow — Page 41

Cannonbolt — Page 13

Four Arms — Page 32

Stinkfly — Page 55

Heatblast — Page 39

Upgrade — Page 52

XLR8 — Page 50

Size guide

BEN TENNYSON

Our hero is ten years old. When the Omnitrix blasted down to Earth Ben found it and it's been strapped to his wrist ever since. He is now the wielder of one of the most powerful devices in the universe.

Ben's full name is Benjamin Kirby Tennyson.

Ben is terrified of squids!

He is on a mission to collect all the Sumo Slammer cards.

He loves jokes, pranks and teasing his cousin Gwen.

Not a fan of chores, but will do anything for his Grandpa Max.

GWEN

Gwen is Ben's cousin. She's smart and her quick-thinking often helps Ben when he gets into trouble. She's always got Ben's back and despite their differences they make a great team.

Gwen loves facts and knows a lot about EVERYTHING!

She's awesome at computer games and battles with Ben for high scores.

GRANDPA MAX

Grandpa Max owns the Rustbucket, an awesome motor home, which is Ben and Gwen's home for the summer. He loves planning visits to new places, has a huge sense of adventure and love for the Great Outdoors.

Grandpa Max is a BIG fan of long hikes.

He enjoys visiting obscure places, the weirder the better.

Can you spot Grey Matter in the alien line-up?

See answer on page 60.

PACK IT UP!

Time to get ready for the trip of a lifetime. Ben has made a list of his essential summer-trip items to take on the Rustbucket. Read his list, then make your own below.

- ★ Sumo Slammer Cards (Hopefully I'll find even more)
- ★ Computer Games (Gonna need some entertainment)
- ★ Sumo Slammer Comics (Midnight-reading essentials)
- ★ Water Pistol (To annoy Gwen ☺)
- ★ Football (To play with all the friends I'll meet)
- ★ Secret Sweet Stash (Midnight gaming fuel)
- ★ Awesome New Trainers (For all the hikes Grandpa will make us go on 😖)

What are your must-have items for a big trip? List them here:

BEN 10

BEN 10

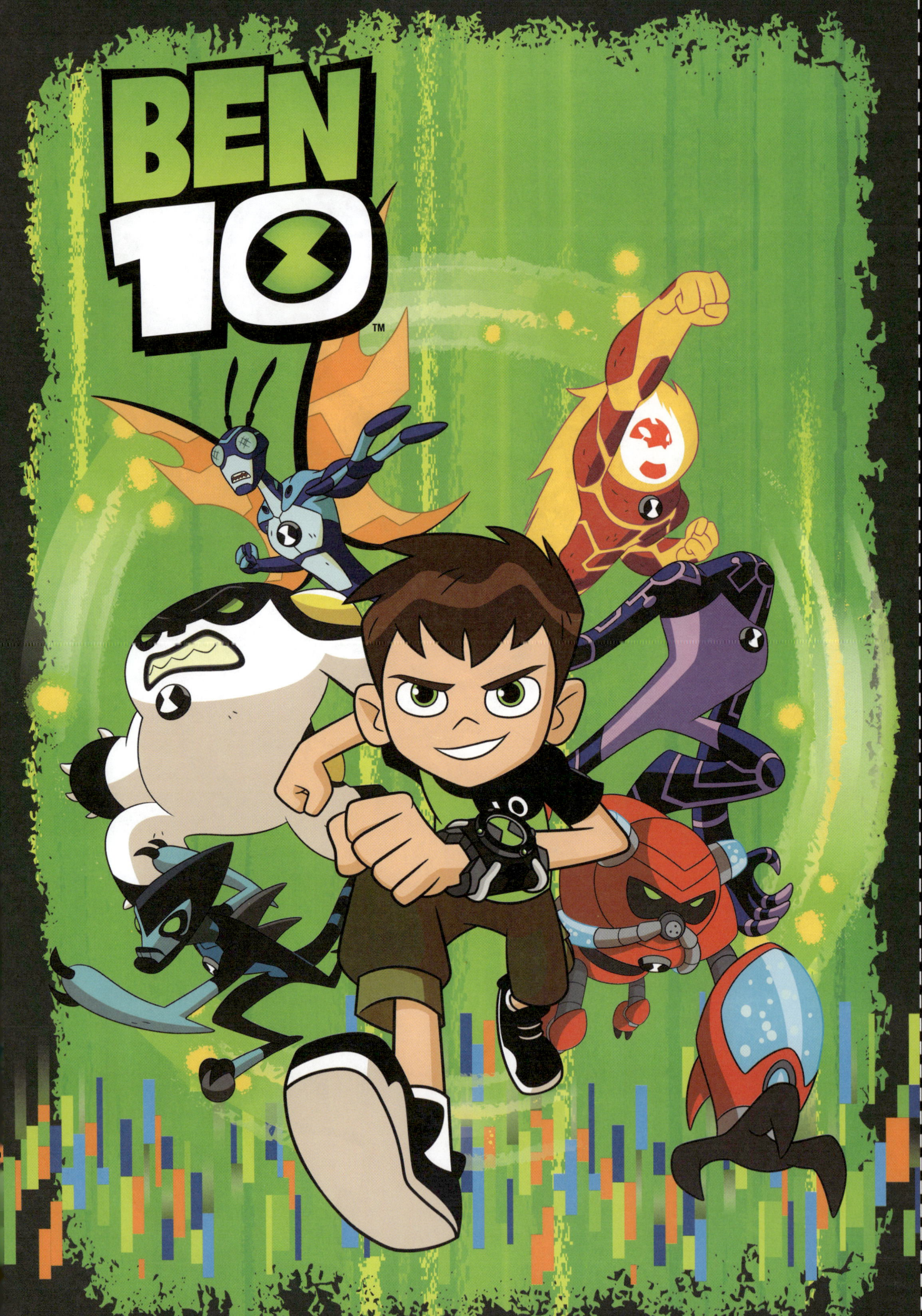

TM & © Cartoon Network. (ss17)

CANNONBOLT FACT FILE

He's big, fierce and you wouldn't want to get in his way. Check out these awesome facts about Cannonbolt.

What's he made of?
Cannonbolt is made of a nearly invulnerable material, which makes him virtually unstoppable.

Power
He can curl himself up into a ball and roll at fast speeds.

DID YOU KNOW?
Cannonbolt comes from a planet called Arburia.

Cannonbolt is way cool!

And big and round!

And he rolls along the ground! Call me a poet.

Watch out!
Sometimes Cannonbolt finds it difficult to stop!

Ball Games

Cannonbolt can turn into an unstoppable ball. Can you name three types of sports balls? Write them in the boxes below.

1. _____ 2. _____ 3. _____

See answers on page 60.

FAMILY SEQUENCES

Check out the family snaps below and work out which picture comes next in the sequences.

A **B** **C**

1. A – B – C – A – B – **?**
2. B – A – B – A – B – **?**
3. A – C – C – A – C – **?**
4. C – A – B – C – A – **?**
5. B – B – A – A – B – **?**

See answers on page 60.

VINE TIME

Wildvine is on the attack. Doodle more vines coming from his body and fill the page with wild power.

Tip: Make sure you don't get his vines in a tangle!

Colour in the frame to complete your masterpiece!

MEGA MATCH-UP TIME

Ben may have stayed up too late watching Sumo Slammer episodes last night, because he's having trouble working out which shadows belong to which Aliens. Help him out and match them up.

1
2
3
4
5
6
7
8
9
10

Answers

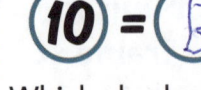

1 = K
2 = M
3 = A
4 = D
5 = L
6 = E
7 = I
8 = C
9 = F
10 = B

Which shadows don't match any Alien?
B H G

See answers on page 60.

16

Tip: There are more shadows here than there are Aliens, so take extra care!

17

CREATE YOUR OWN ALIEN

Have you ever imagined yourself as an Alien? Let your imagination go wild on these pages and create an Omnitrix worthy Alien!

CIRCLE THE WORDS THAT APPLY TO YOUR ALIEN:

▶ **IS IT...?**
BIG
SMALL
SLOW
FAST
SHY
SCARY

▶ **DOES IT HAVE...?**
HORNS
A TAIL
WINGS
A BEAK
BIG FEET

WHAT PLANET IS IT FROM?
_____

THINK UP A FUN NAME AND WRITE IT HERE:
_____

WHAT'S ITS DNA LIKE?

WRITE ABOUT ITS POWER AND SPECIAL ATTACKS HERE.

DRAW YOUR ALIEN HERE:

Label its special features!

COUNTER ATTACK!

WHOA! There are so many Alien counters on these pages. Count them up and write their totals on the right. Once you're done, answer the questions around the page!

Which Alien appears the most?

Design your own counter in this circle!

20

BEN 10

Which Alien appears the least?

Which Alien appears ten times?

Alien	Count
Ben 10	
Omnitrix	
Upgrade	
Heatblast	
Overflow	
Diamondhead	
Wildvine	
Cannonbolt	
XLR8	
Four Arms	
Grey Matter	13
Stinkfly	

See answers on page 60.

CROSSWORD ALIENS

Solve the clues below to complete this Alien-themed word puzzle.

ACROSS

1. With skin of liquid metal, this Alien can boost and power technology.
5. His DNA is silicon-based and diamond hard.
8. Blink and you'll miss this speedy Alien.
9. Things tend to heat up when this Alien is around.
10. Shoots water from his arms like water pistols.

DOWN

2. The smallest but by no means the weakest Alien in Ben's line-up.
3. Can roll himself into an unstoppable ball.
4. Why have two when you can have four?
6. Keep away from this Alien's flammable goo and slime attack!
7. Baddies often get tangled up in this Alien's attacks.

See answers on page 60.

CODED QUESTION

You're going to need all your brainpower to solve this one!

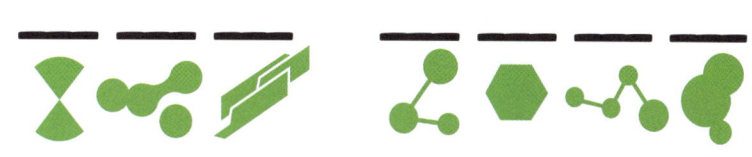

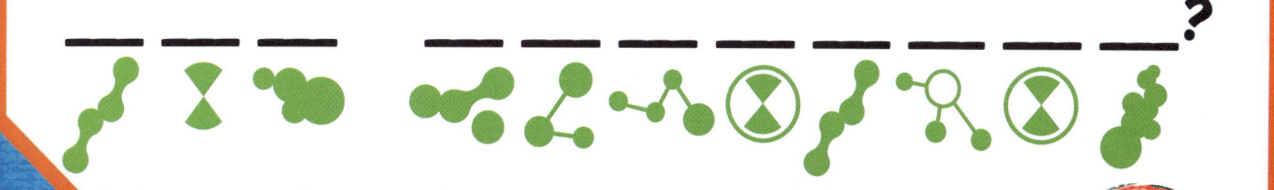

Grey Matter is testing your Ben 10 knowledge, but he's not making it easy for you because he's testing you in code. Use the symbols to work out what he's asking you, then answer his question.

WHO ATE ONE OF BEN'S SANDWICHES?

Answer

DIAMONDHEAD FACT FILE

He's shiny, he's big and he's hero ready. Check out these awesome facts about Diamondhead.

What's he made of?
His body is made of green crystals.

DNA
It's silicone-based and diamond hard.

Power
Ben can control Diamondhead's structure and reform it into crystal weapons, from swords to shields.

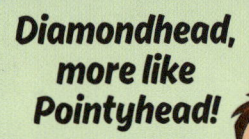

Diamondhead, more like Pointyhead!

I'd watch out who you call pointy head!

DID YOU KNOW?

Diamondhead comes from a planet called Petropia.

Gem Test

Diamondhead has a gem-inspired name. Can you name three other precious gems? Write them in the boxes below.

1.
2.
3.

See answers on page 60.

CODED COLOURING

Use the code to colour in the Omnitrix and make it look super awesome.

Code

1, 2, 3, 4, 5, 6

COLOURING TIP

To get a different shade of grey, try pressing harder or lighter with your pencil.

DID YOU KNOW?

Ben found the Omnitrix after it crashed to Earth from space!

POWERS OF OBSERVATION

Villains beware! Ben and Gwen have become really good at spotting when something or someone is up to no good. Test your powers of observation in these spot-the-difference challenges!

CHALLENGE ONE:

EASY

Can you find the **five** differences between these two pictures?

CHALLENGE TWO:

MEDIUM

Now, can you find the **five** differences between these two pictures?

26

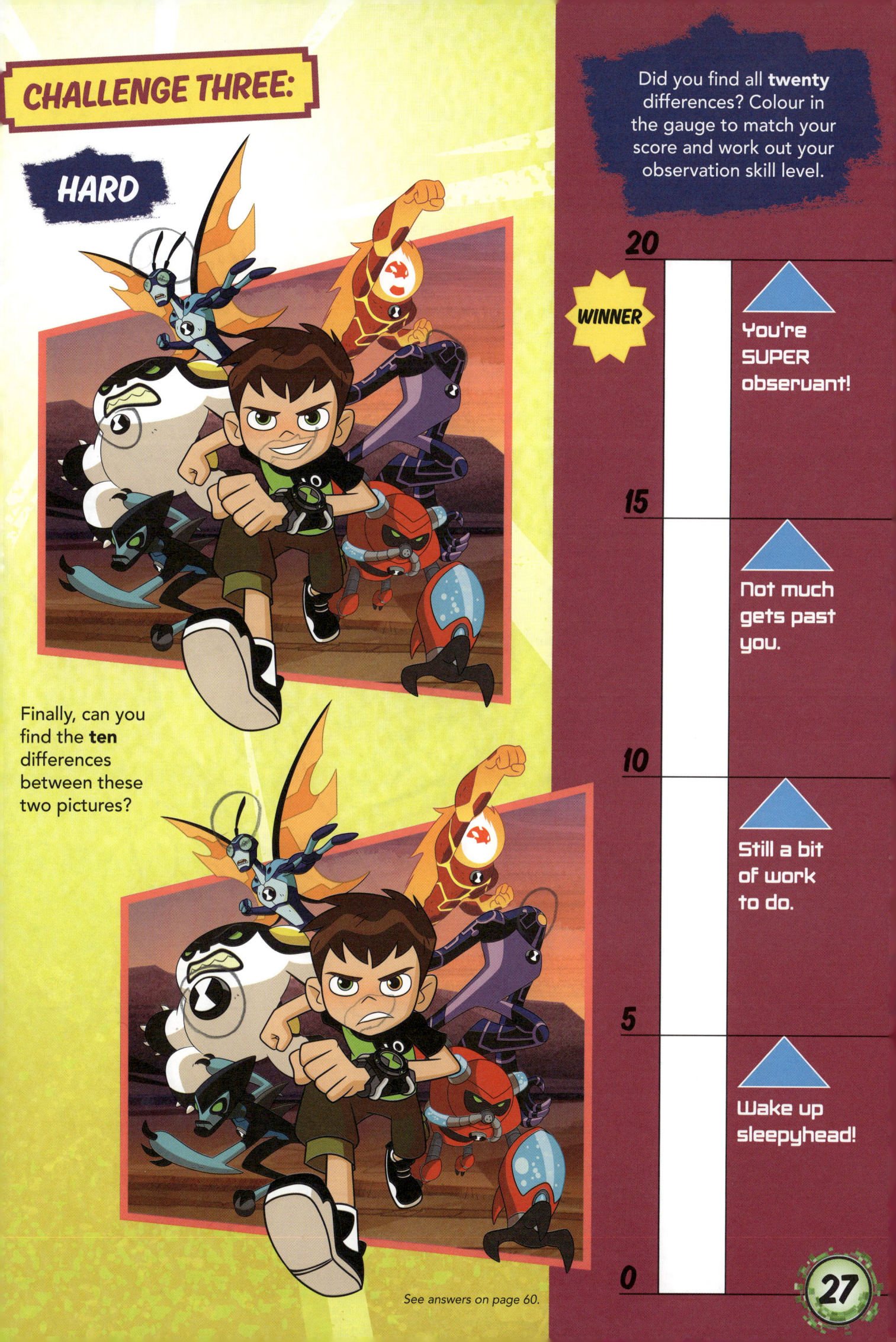

CHALLENGE THREE:

HARD

Finally, can you find the **ten** differences between these two pictures?

Did you find all **twenty** differences? Colour in the gauge to match your score and work out your observation skill level.

20

WINNER

▲ You're SUPER observant!

15

▲ Not much gets past you.

10

▲ Still a bit of work to do.

5

▲ Wake up sleepyhead!

0

See answers on page 60.

27

ACTION COLOURING

Check out this awesome battle scene between Four Arms and some mean-looking villains. Make the pages pop by colouring in the pictures.

WATCH OUT, FOUR ARMS!

THAT'S A POWERFUL ATTACK!

DODGE AND PUNCH!

29

COMIC CREATOR

Imagine you're the star of your very own Ben 10 adventure. Write, draw and create your own comic-strip story below.

ONE DAY, I WAS IN THE ... *(TICK THE BOX)*
- ☐ CLASSROOM
- ☐ WOODS
- ☐ SUPERMARKET

WHEN AN EVIL VILLAIN CALLED _____ SHOWED UP AND...

DRAW THE VILLAIN HERE!

EVERYONE RAN AWAY BECAUSE... *(WHAT DID THE VILLAIN DO?)*
_____
_____
_____
_____
_____

I SUMMONED _____ FROM THE OMNITRIX. IT WAS TIME TO BATTLE!

DRAW THE ALIEN HERE!

30

THE BATTLE WAS TOUGH, BUT I USED A SPECIAL POWER.

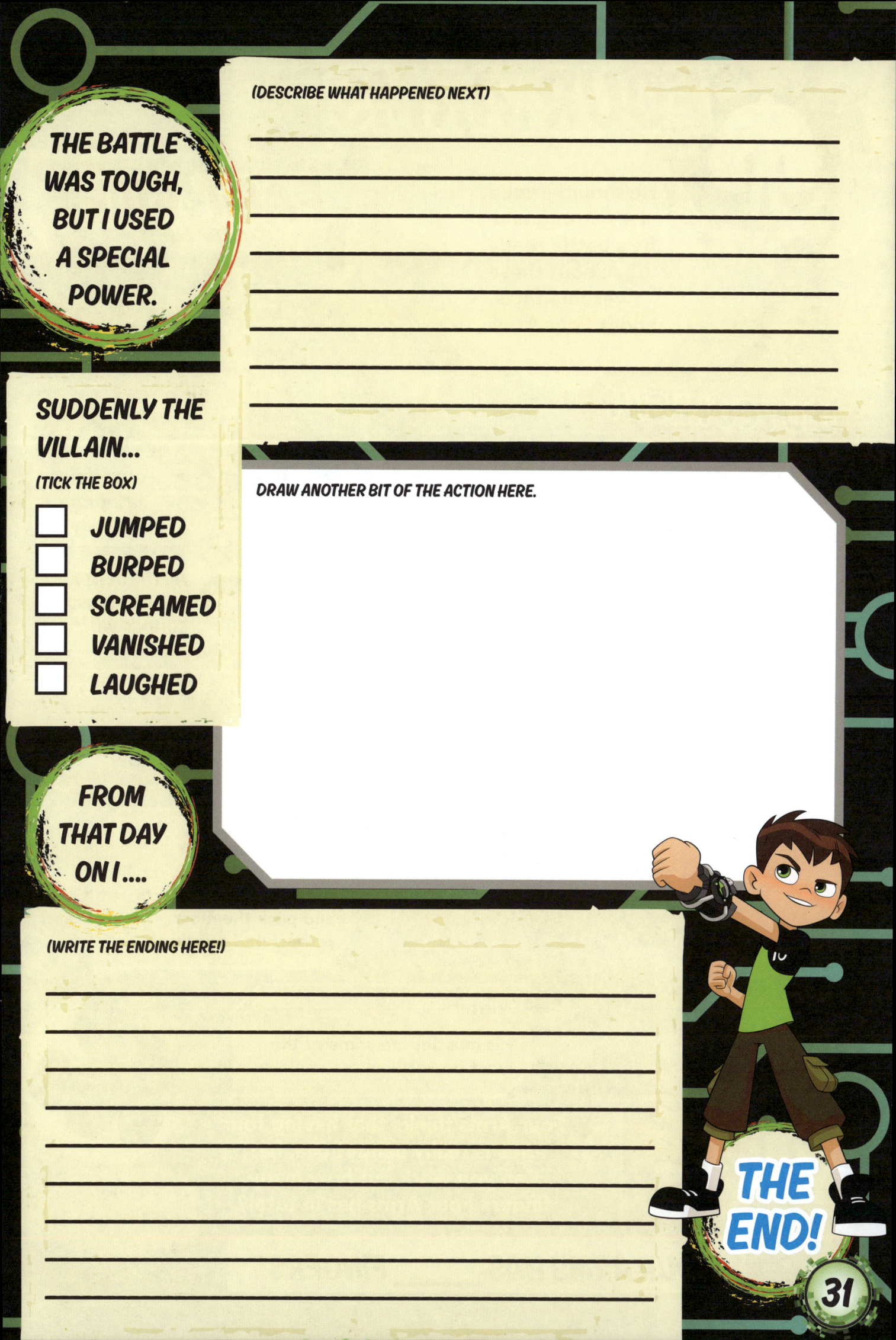

(DESCRIBE WHAT HAPPENED NEXT)

_____
_____
_____
_____
_____
_____
_____

SUDDENLY THE VILLAIN...
(TICK THE BOX)

- ☐ JUMPED
- ☐ BURPED
- ☐ SCREAMED
- ☐ VANISHED
- ☐ LAUGHED

DRAW ANOTHER BIT OF THE ACTION HERE.

FROM THAT DAY ON I....

(WRITE THE ENDING HERE!)

_____
_____
_____
_____
_____
_____
_____

THE END!

FOUR ARMS FACT FILE

He's multi-armed, he's strong and he's battle ready. Check out these awesome facts about Four Arms.

DID YOU KNOW?

Four Arms comes from a planet called Khoros.

Four stinky armpits, ewwwwww!

All the better to make gross sounds with!

What's he made of?
His body is made up of pure Alien muscle. POW!

Power
As Four Arms, Ben can lift the heaviest of objects and pack the most powerful of punches.

Watch Out!
His muscles are some of the most powerful in the universe.

The Power of Four

Four Arms thinks that having four arms is really handy! (Ha, ha!) Can you work out how many fingers Four Arms has in total?

Clue: It's 4+4+4+4!

FOUR ARMS HAS _____ FINGERS!

See answers on page 61.

CAMPSITE CONFUSION

Look at this campsite picture of Ben, Gwen and Grandpa Max. Some of the pieces are missing. Can you work out which pieces complete the picture?

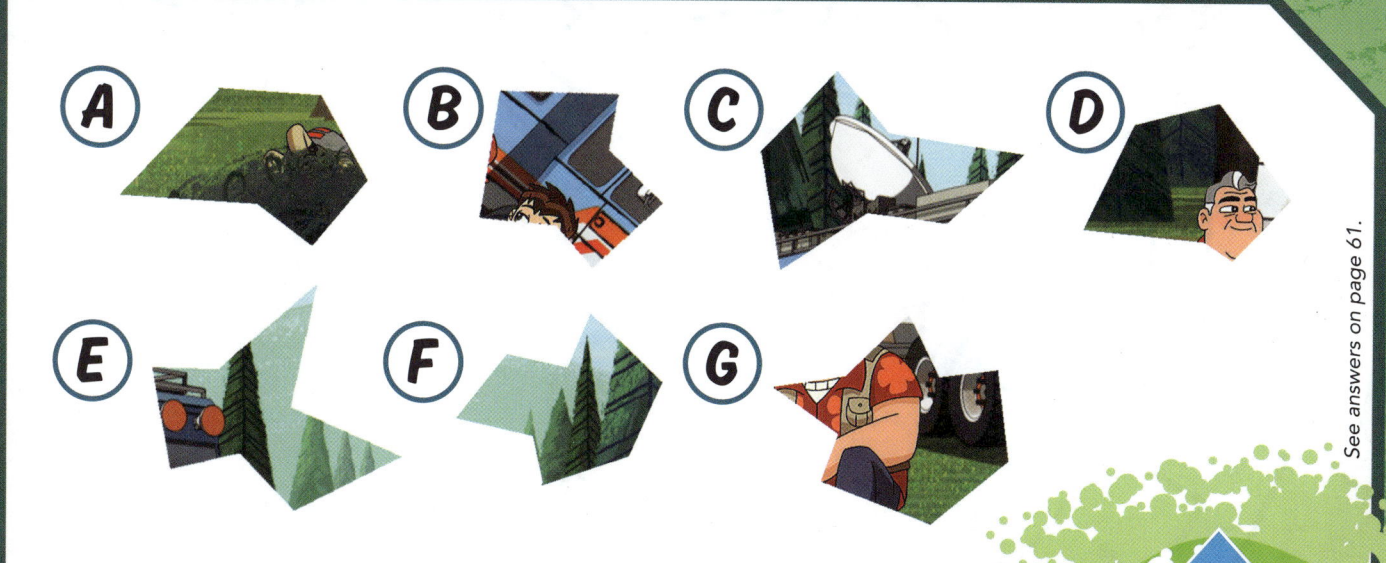

Answers

1 = ◯
2 = ◯
3 = ◯
4 = ◯

Is there someone spying on Ben?

33

FLAMING MAZE

There's only one Alien that can cool down this sizzling situation. Help Overflow find a path through the maze avoiding the hot spots and stop La Grange from making his escape!

DID YOU KNOW?

La Grange is obsessed with treasure and will do anything to get it, no matter what the cost.

FINISH

35

See answers on page 61.

GREY MATTER FACT FILE

He's tiny, he's mighty and he's ready for anything. Check out these awesome facts about Grey Matter.

DID YOU KNOW?

Grey Matter comes from a planet called Galvan Prime.

What's he made of?
Grey Matter is very similar to a frog.

Power
Grey Matter is a tech head, able to see how complex machines work by literally getting inside them.

Watch out!
Despite his small size, he has incredible strength!

Small, but mighty intelligent!

Hmm, one tenth intelligent you mean.

I'll take it!

Brain-teaser

Here is a riddle to test your brain cells.

What is as light as a feather, but impossible to hold for more than a few minutes?

See answer on page 61.

MUDDLE TROUBLE

Help Four Arms get a grip on this villain by working out which steamed-up line will lead him to Steam Smythe.

1 2 3

Gwen

Steam Smythe

Grandpa Max

OUT OF THIS WORLD JOKES

Ben is known to face his enemies with a lot of fun and humour. Read these HA-HA-Larious Alien-inspired jokes and see if you can't help but crack a smile.

What do you call an alien with three eyes?
An aliiiien!

Where do aliens go to school?
Universe-ities!

What's an alien's favourite dance?
Moonwalk

What do you call a spaceship that's upset?
A crying saucer!

What do aliens like to drink?
A nice cup of Gravi-tea!

What do aliens like to read?
Comet Books

How do you get an alien to sleep?
Rocket

What do you say to a two-headed alien?
Hello! Hello!

What do aliens wear to the office?
Space suits!

HEATBLAST FACT FILE

He's bright, he's blasty and he's flaming hot. Check out these awesome facts about Heatblast.

DID YOU KNOW?

Heatblast comes from a planet called Pyros.

DNA
His DNA is comprised of a magma-like substance that is incredibly hot.

Power
Ben has control over all heat-based blasts and is able to throw fire from his hands.

Watch Out!
Heatblast's flame can be put out with water.

Heatblast can also burp flames.

And make popcorn in two seconds!

The Heat is On!

Fill in the missing letters on these hot words.

F L _ M E
_ U R N
B _ I L

See answers on page 61.

RUSTY DOT-TO-DOT

Grandpa Max's love for the outdoors is probably only matched by his love of the trusty Rustbucket. Complete this dot-to-dot of his beloved truck!

START

END

Once you're done, colour it and draw a scene around it!

You could give the Rustbucket a new colourful makeover for fun.

OVERFLOW

He's aqua-powered, he's strong and he's ready to make a splash. Check out these awesome facts about Overflow.

FACT FILE

DID YOU KNOW?
Overflow comes from a planet called Kiusana.

What's he made of?
This alien is a mysterious, liquid-based creature.

Power
Ben has control over most forms of moisture and can shoot water from his arms.

And no known weaknesses.

Is being annoying a weakness?

I'd consider it a strength!

Watch Out!
When you can control water, you can control most of the planet!

Ocean Challenge

Can you name three large oceans?

1. _____
2. _____
3. _____

See answers on page 61.

41

STORY

THE FILTH

1. Out in the desert, something stinky was going down.

2. The Bug Brothers, Maurice and Sydney, were stealing nuclear waste from a truck.

3. "We nearly have enough waste! But we need more... Hmm, do you smell that?" said Maurice, sniffing the air.

Hmm, do you smell that?

4. Meanwhile nearby, Gwen, Grandpa Max and Ben were having a spring clean.

5. They had been cleaning for hours. "Something still stinks!" said Gwen, puzzled.

6. It was Ben. He hadn't cleaned at all. He'd been streaming his favourite TV show instead!

7. "No wifi until you've done your chores," said Grandpa Max as he left with Gwen to go on a hike.

No wifi until you've done your chores.

8. "No problemo!" thought Ben. All he needed to get the job done was some Alien intervention.

No problemo!

9. But trouble was nearby. The Bug Brothers had followed their noses and hatched a plan to steal the stinky Rustbucket.

42

10 Sydney smacked an unsuspecting XLR8 and the Bug Brothers sped away in their stinky prize.

11 Of course it didn't take XLR8 long to catch up… or be hit again, this time by nuclear sludge. Gross!

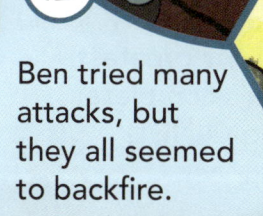

12 Ben tried many attacks, but they all seemed to backfire.

13 And when the Omnitrix ran out of juice, Ben hit the road the old-fashioned way, by foot.

14 Ben followed the Rustbucket's tracks to a nuclear waste facility. It was a really lovely place.

15 OK, it really wasn't. But Ben did make a great discovery – the Rustbucket had been cleaned tyre to roof!

16 All the waste had been pumped into a mysterious machine. What were those Bug Brothers up to?

17 Ben knew it couldn't be anything good. It was probably time for him to start punching things.

18 But before he could throw a punch, Maurice did some punching of his own, punching a button to activate the waste machine!

43

THE FILTH CONTINUED...

20 "Thanks to your disgusting habits..."

19 "It's FULLY FUNCTIONAL, SYDNEY! My greatest invention is complete! The Magg-O-NET!" cried Maurice.

20 Then something total yuck happened. A zillion maggots zoomed towards the machine.

21 "Thanks to your disgusting habits, I've reached the final phase of my master plan," Maurice taunted Ben.

22 The maggots formed a monster. The Magg-O-NET Monster. It was grosser than Ben's unwashed underpants. And it liked to eat ANYTHING!

CRUNCH!

23 "Do you see Las Vegas over there?"

"Do you see Las Vegas over there?!?! I want you to eat everything except the money!" Maurice ordered the monster.

24 "So, let me get this straight?"

"So, let me get this straight? You stole our motor home, so you could fuel that trash machine to power a magnet that attracts maggots to make a monster that would eat Las Vegas? Whatever. Time to throw stuff!"

44

25 Ben crunched and smashed the remote control…

26 …but that was a big mistake. Now the monster was out of control.

27 The Bug Brothers crawled away scared, leaving Ben to deal with the monster.

28 Ben realised there was a magnet powering the monster. He threw the Rustbucket…

WHAM!

29 …and WHAM, the magnet was blasted away.

30 "Ha, ha!" thought Ben. "Now I get it. Maggot, Magg-O-NET!"

31 There was still one problem, though. The Rustbucket was now covered in maggots. Ben set to work and the Rustbucket was sparkling by the time Gwen and Grandpa Max got back. Grandpa was pleased.

32 "You did a great job cleaning, but you have to finish all your chores before you get your wifi back." Grandpa Max told him.

"Oh man!"

THE END

HIDDEN HEX

One of these pictures of Overflow is not like the others. In fact, Ben suspects that one of them is Hex in disguise. Can you spot Hex?

Use this Hex picture to help you.

Eye spy that something's not right!

46 See answer on page 61.

WILDVINE

He's wild, he's green and he's mean. Check out these awesome facts about Wildvine.

FACT FILE

DID YOU KNOW?
Wildvine comes from a planet called Flors Verdance.

What's he made of?
Awesome adaptable plant material.

Watch Out!
Ben has to be careful not to get his vines tangled up.

That collar is the height of Flors Verdance fashion!

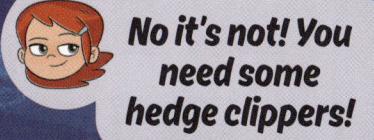

No it's not! You need some hedge clippers!

Power
Ben can merge with any plant on the planet and can grow and retract arms and vines at will.

Plant Life

Can you name the type of forest that is home to most of the world's species of plants (and animals!)? Fill in the missing letters.

| _ | A | _ | N | _ | O R E _ T |

See answer on page 61.

47

TRAVELLING TRIO

Ben, Gwen and Grandpa Max are on the road again on their way to a cool campsite. (Well, Ben and Gwen hope it is!) Help Grandpa Max navigate the best route for the Rustbucket, avoiding the villains along the way.

START

CONTINUE

See answers on page 61.

XLR8

He's super-sonic, he's strong and he's ready to race. Check out these awesome facts about XLR8.

FACT FILE

DID YOU KNOW?
XLR8 comes from a planet called Kinet.

What's he made of?
He's made of matter which can tolerate 500 mph speeds.

Watch Out!
XLR8 better be fast, as strength is not a strong suit for this alien form.

Power
Ben is the super speedster alien and can travel at crazy high speeds!

Why do you have bowling feet?

Why do you always act like a baby?

I don't act like a baby. I don't I don't I don't!

Animal Speed

Fill in the missing letters to reveal the name of the speediest Earth animal on land.

Did you know that this animal can run at over 60 mph?

C H E _ T _ H

50

See answers on page 61.

POWER OF TEN WORDSEARCH

Ben has listed 10 words that are important to him. Can you find them in the grid below? Look across, down and diagonally!

ACTION
ADVENTURE
ALIEN
BATTLE
FAMILY
FUN
HERO
OMNITRIX
POWER
TEN

J	B	A	T	T	L	E	G	A	D	T	Y
W	Z	O	Q	A	U	K	R	F	P	H	C
A	M	S	E	T	C	V	X	U	B	E	F
J	D	H	N	W	I	T	E	N	Q	R	D
P	S	V	H	U	M	A	I	K	L	O	W
A	L	I	E	N	Y	Z	K	O	F	T	B
M	D	A	R	N	U	X	F	J	N	L	E
G	O	M	N	I	T	R	I	X	O	V	P
T	K	R	C	S	H	U	B	A	D	F	O
X	O	Q	F	K	N	E	R	G	Y	P	W
J	F	A	M	I	L	Y	T	E	X	I	E
Y	V	L	B	A	O	L	C	S	U	K	R

Can you write down ten words that are important to you?

1. TEN
2. BATTLE
3. ____
4. ____
5. Love
6. your
7. I
8. are
9. found
10. ____

See answers on page 61.

51

UPGRADE

He's mysterious, he's adaptable and he's ready to take charge. Check out these awesome facts about Upgrade.

FACT FILE

DID YOU KNOW?
Upgrade comes from a moon called Galvan.

Upgrade's colours are violet and indigo.

Don't you mean purple and purple?!

What's he made of?
Upgrade is a "mechamorph" – a living machine with liquid metallic skin.

Power
His nanotechnological body can pour itself over any piece of technology, merge with it and upgrade it to something more powerful.

Upgrade the Rustbucket

Doodle and colour Upgrade's skin patterns over this picture of the Rustbucket!

52

BEN 10

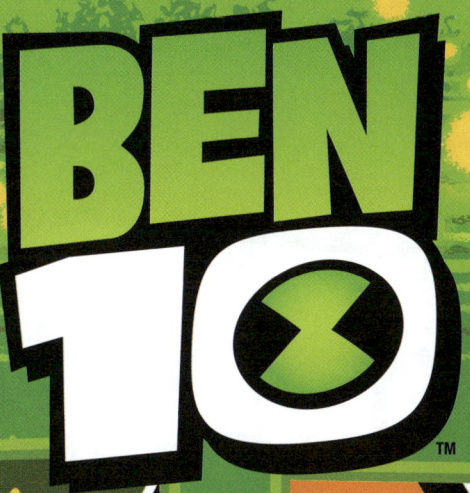

BEN 10

STINKFLY

He's fast, he can fly and he's ready to make a stink. Check out these awesome facts about Stinkfly.

FACT FILE

DID YOU KNOW?
Stinkfly comes from a planet called Lepidopterra.

Power
The liquid goos and gases he shoots from his eyes and mouth possess a wide range of powers.

What's he made of?
Stinkfly is similar to a glowing insect.

Watch Out!
Some of the goo is highly flammable!

I'm not sure Stinkfly smells any worse than your old underwear.

Let's do a test... on you!

Buzz Off!
Fill in the missing letters on these buzzy insects' names.

W _ SP
_ UMBL _ B _ E
D _ AGONFLY

See answers on page 61.

STORY

RUSTBUCKET RIP

1. Ben and Gwen were not too pumped by the thought of visiting Oldeville.

2. Although Ben perked up when he spotted a shop selling a rare Sumo Slammer Card.

3. *Can we go? Can we go? Can we go?* "Can we go? Can we go? Can we go?" Ben cried. "Maybe later," replied Grandpa Max, "I've got a whole list of things planned."

4. *No way!* "No way! I need that card – there's only one!" said Ben.

5. "Tell you what, Ben, you can either spend the day exploring Oldeville, not using your powers, or spend the day doing chores, not using your powers."

6. "Chores, please!" said Ben. "Me too!" said Gwen.

7. Grandpa Max went off on his first tour of the day. Instantly Ben transformed into XLR8.

8. *That's cheating, Ben!* "That's cheating, Ben!" said Gwen. "I'll be back soon – gotta collect me a card!" said Ben.

9. Someone else was also speeding after the card...the youngest super-villain in the world. Billy Billions!

10 Ben beat Billy to the shop and got the card! What a result!

11 *I want that card!*
But Billy wasn't happy about it. "I want that card," cried Billy. "And I always get what I want!"

12 Ben wouldn't give it up, so Billy decided to steal the Rustbucket.

13 Bad timing! Grandpa Max was returning from a tour.

14 Gwen and Ben needed to distract Grandpa Max fast. So they hopped on another tour with him.

15 *I'm going to go and do something.*
"I'm going to go and do something," said Ben, sneaking off the bus and changing into Wildvine.

16 *It's wild time!*
Ben had spotted Billy driving away. "It's wild time!" he cried, chasing after Billy.

17 Using his vine attack, Ben closed in on the Rustbucket.

18 *Time to test out my special tech attacks!*
But Billy was prepared. "Time to test out my special tech attacks!" said Billy, activating a panel.

57

RUSTBUCKET RIP CONTINUED...

19 "Dodge this if you can! It's the best tech that money can buy!"

20 Wildvine struggled with Billy's machine, but crushed it with his plant power.

21 Luckily Grandpa Max didn't notice as Ben sped by!

22 With the Omnitrix out of juice, Ben ducked inside the Rustbucket.

23 He zapped Billy's tech with water – if only he could turn into Overflow!

24 When the Omnitrix recharged, Ben called out "Overflow!" but he got Heatblast instead.

25 Billy was ready to strike again and sent more tech Ben's way.

26 "Why do I never get the Alien I really need?" said Ben, as Billy attacked again.

27 Ben spotted a fire hydrant and blasted it! Water burst out and destroyed the tech.

28

29

Billy was so annoyed that he started to blast up the town. "I may not like this town," said Ben, "but you really need to stop that now!"

Ben blasted Billy's car and the legs began to break.

30

I JUST WANT THAT CARD!

31

32

Finally, Heatblast zapped Billy's car in two.

Billy threw a tantrum. "I JUST WANT THAT CARD," he bawled.

Things only got worse for Billy when his super-villain parents turned up.

I have the perfect solution.

33

34

I will get my revenge!

"So all of this was about a card?" said Grandpa Max. "I have the perfect solution." He ripped the card in two.

"I will get my revenge!" cried Billy as his parents dragged him away.

35 "Looks like we'll be staying in Oldeville until the Rustbucket is fixed," said Gwen. "Please don't make me go to the Dust Museum!" said Ben.

Please don't make me go to the Dust Museum!

THE END

ANSWERS

P 5
Sumo Slammer cards are on pages: 8, 10, 16, 25, 30, 34, 38, 46, 49, 57.

P 8
Grey Matter is here.

P 13
Did you get any of these suggestions?
FOOTBALL, TENNIS BALL, PING-PONG BALL, GOLF BALL, BASKETBALL, NETBALL, SNOOKER BALL, BOWLING BALL, BASEBALL, to name a few …

P 14
1. C;   2. A;   3. C;   4. B;   5. B.

P 16
1. = K;   2. = M;   3. = A;   4. = D;
5. = L;   6. = E;   7. = I;   8. = C;
9. = F;   10. = B
The shadows that don't match any Aliens are: G, H, J.

P 20-21

Ben 10	4
X	6
	7
	5
	2
	6
	10
	9
	7
	3
	13
	4

Grey Matter appears the most.
Overflow appears the least.
Wildvine appears ten times.

P 22

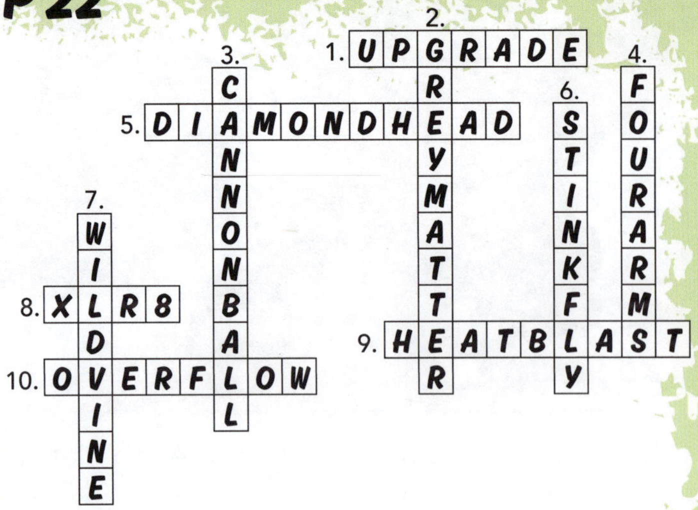

Crossword:
1. UPGRADE
2. (down)
3. CANNONBALL
4. FOURARMS
5. DIAMONDHEAD
6. STINKFLY
7. WIDEVINE
8. XLR8
9. HEATBLAST
10. OVERFLOW
(down clue: GREYMATTER)

P 23
How many Aliens are in the Omnitrix?
Answer: 10.

P 24
Did you get any of these suggestions?
RUBY, SAPPHIRE, EMERALD.

P 26-27
1. Easy 
2. Medium 
3. Hard

P 32
Four Arms has sixteen fingers!

P 33
1. C; 2. E; 3. G; 4. A.
Dr Amino is spying on Ben.

P 34-35

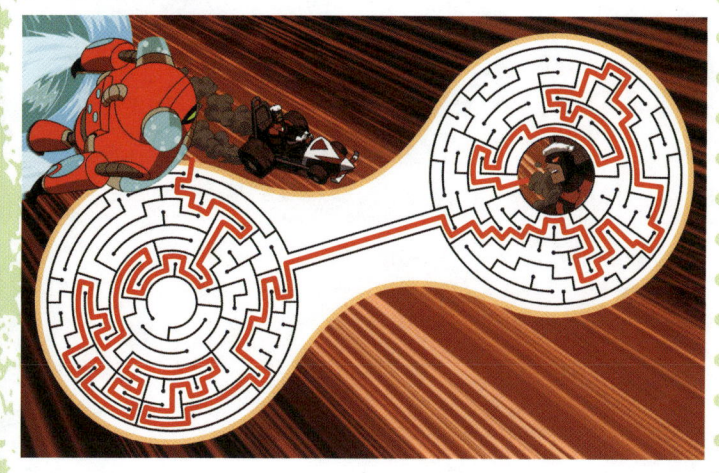

P 36
"Your breath!"

P 37
Line 3 leads to Steam Smythe.

P 39
FLAME
BURN
BOIL

P 41
The Pacific Ocean, Atlantic Ocean, Southern Ocean, Indian Ocean, Arctic Ocean.

P 46
Overflow 4. is Hex in disguise.

P 47
RAINFOREST

P 48-49

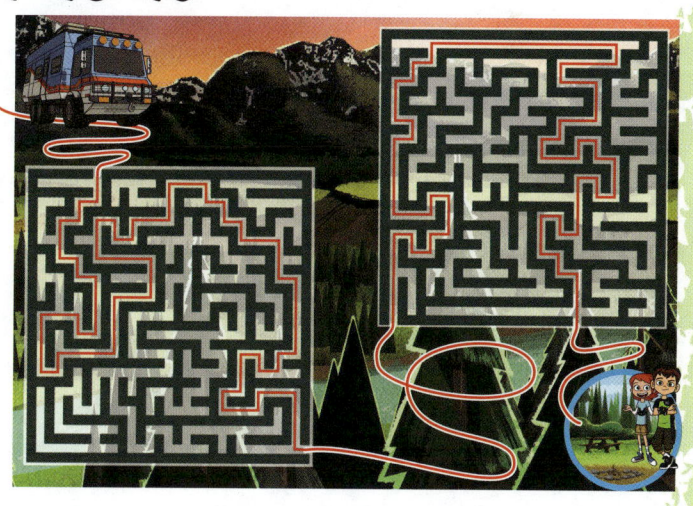

P 50
CHEETAH

P 51

P 55
WASP
BUMBLEBEE
DRAGONFLY

61